First World War
and Army of Occupation
War Diary
France, Belgium and Germany

15 DIVISION
Divisional Troops
73 Brigade Royal Field Artillery
4 July 1915 - 2 December 1916

WO95/1924/2

The Naval & Military Press Ltd
www.nmarchive.com
Published in association with The National Archives

Published by

The Naval & Military Press Ltd

Unit 10 Ridgewood Industrial Park,

Uckfield, East Sussex,

TN22 5QE England

Tel: +44 (0) 1825 749494

www.naval-military-press.com

www.nmarchive.com

This diary has been reprinted in facsimile from the original. Any imperfections are inevitably reproduced and the quality may fall short of modern type and cartographic standards.

© **Crown Copyright**
Images reproduced by permission of The National Archives, London, England, 2015.

Contents

Document type	Place/Title	Date From	Date To
Heading	WO95/1924/2		
Heading	15th Division 73rd Brigade R.F.A. Jly 1915-Dec 1916 Broken J A Box 1924		
Heading	15th Division 73rd Brigade R.F.A. Vol I		
War Diary	Bulford	04/07/1915	08/07/1915
War Diary	Southampton	08/07/1915	08/07/1915
War Diary	Havre	09/07/1915	10/07/1915
War Diary	Audruicq	11/07/1915	11/07/1915
War Diary	Bonningues	15/07/1915	15/07/1915
War Diary	Campagne	16/07/1915	16/07/1915
War Diary	Guarbecque	17/07/1915	17/07/1915
War Diary	Lapugnoy	29/07/1915	29/07/1915
Heading	15th Division "B"/73 Battery. R.F.A. Vol I. Nil 7-28-7-15		
War Diary	Bulford	07/07/1915	07/07/1915
War Diary	Southampton	08/07/1915	08/07/1915
War Diary	Le Havre	09/07/1915	09/07/1915
War Diary	St Omer	11/07/1915	28/07/1915
War Diary	15th Division 73rd Bde. R.F.A. Vol II August 15		
War Diary	Le Brebis	02/08/1915	03/08/1915
War Diary	Noeux-Les-Mines	07/08/1915	30/08/1915
Heading	15th Division B/73 Battery Vol II August 15		
War Diary	Les Brebis	01/08/1915	28/08/1915
Heading	War Diary 73rd Brigade. R.F.A. (15th Division) September 1915		
War Diary	Mazingarbe	02/09/1915	30/09/1915
Heading	15th Division 73rd Bde. R.F.A. Vol. 4 Oct 15		
War Diary	Mazingarbe	01/10/1915	31/10/1915
Heading	15th Division 73rd Bde R.F.A. Vol. 15 Nov 15		
War Diary	Vermelles	01/11/1915	30/11/1915
Heading	15th Div 73rd Bde. R.F.A. Vol 6		
War Diary		01/12/1915	21/12/1915
War Diary	Cluchel	22/12/1915	31/12/1915
Miscellaneous	War Diary of 73rd Brigade Royal Field Arty From 1st September, 1916 to 30th September, 1916 Volume 15		
Heading	73rd Bde. R.F.A. Vol:7		
War Diary	Auchel	01/01/1916	16/01/1916
War Diary	Les. Brebis	17/01/1916	29/02/1916
Heading	73 R.F.A. Vol 9		
War Diary	Les Brebis	01/03/1916	26/04/1916
War Diary	Lieres.	27/04/1916	28/04/1916
War Diary	Lieres Bethune	29/04/1916	29/04/1916
War Diary	Bethune	30/04/1916	30/04/1916
Heading	War Diary B/73rd Brigade R.F.A. 30th April to 8th June 1916		
War Diary	G I.B Central	30/04/1916	08/06/1916
War Diary	Bethune	01/05/1916	31/05/1916
Heading	War Diary D/73rd Brigade R.F.A. May 1916		
War Diary	Amiequin	01/05/1916	31/05/1916
War Diary	Bethune	01/06/1916	30/06/1916

Heading	War Diary B/73rd Brigade R.F.A. June 1916		
War Diary	Annequin	07/06/1916	17/06/1916
War Diary	Ammequin & Vermelles	18/06/1916	30/06/1916
Heading	War Diary 73rd Bde R.F.A. From 1st to 31st July. 1916.		
War Diary	Bethune	01/07/1916	05/07/1916
War Diary	Bethune-Philosophe	05/07/1916	06/07/1916
War Diary	Philosophe	06/07/1916	31/07/1916
Heading	15th Divisional Artillery 73rd Brigade Royal Field Artillery August 1916		
Heading	War Diary 73rd Brigade, R.F.A. From 1st August, 1916 to 31st August, 1916 Volume number 14		
War Diary	Bethune Court St Ouen	01/08/1916	02/08/1916
War Diary	Beaucourt	02/08/1916	04/08/1916
War Diary	Bazentin	04/08/1916	07/08/1916
War Diary	Mametz	08/08/1916	10/09/1916
War Diary	Peake Woods	11/09/1916	19/09/1916
War Diary	St Gratien	20/09/1916	30/09/1916
Heading	War Diary of 73rd Bde R.F.A. 1st October, 1916. to 31st October, 1916 Volume. 16		
War Diary	St Gratien	01/10/1916	02/10/1916
War Diary	St Gratien Bazentin Le Petit	03/10/1916	03/10/1916
War Diary	Bazentin Le Petit	04/10/1916	31/10/1916
Heading	15 D.A.	30/11/1916	30/11/1916
Heading	War Diary of 73 Bde R.F.A. From 1st November, 1916-30th November, 1916. Volume 17		
War Diary	St Gratien	01/11/1916	09/11/1916
War Diary	Middle Wood	09/11/1916	30/11/1916
Heading	15th D.A. Confidential	03/07/1916	03/07/1916
War Diary	Middle Wood	01/12/1916	02/12/1916

3095/1924(2)

4095/1924(2)

15TH DIVISION

73RD BRIGADE R.F.A.
JLY 1915 - DEC 1916

BROKEN J A

Box 1924

121/6200

15th Division

73rd Brigade 1074.
Vol I

mi 4-29-7-15

away 16

Army Form C. 2118.

WAR DIARY
or
INTELLIGENCE SUMMARY.

(Erase heading not required.)

Instructions regarding War Diaries and Intelligence Summaries are contained in F. S. Regs., Part II. and the Staff Manual respectively. Title pages will be prepared in manuscript.

Place	Date	Hour	Summary of Events and Information	Remarks and references to Appendices
BULFORD	4/7/15	10.30am	Received orders to mobilize	
BULFORD	8/7/15	12.35pm	Entrained for Southampton	
SOUTHAMPTON	8.7.15	7.45pm	Embarked & Sailed on the SS PETERSBURG	
HAVRE	9.7.15	2am	Arrived Stayed one day at No 5 Rest Camp	
HAVRE	10.7.15	3.30pm	Entrained & departed from HAVRE	
AUDRUICQ	11.7.15	9am	Detrained marched to BONNINGUES - Remained in Billets	
BONNINGUES	15.7.15	8am	marched from there to CAMPAGNE stayed in Billets	
CAMPAGNE	16.7.15	8am	marched to GUARBECQUE stayed in Billets	
GUARBECQUE	17.7.15	9am	marched to LAPUGNOY stayed in Billets till 29.7.15	
LAPUGNOY	29/7/15		marched to LE BREBIS & took up position in action. July one Battery in position (B/113) Remained in position. Reserve.	

Certified Correct

[signature]

121/6300

15th Division

"B"/73 Battery R.F.A.

Vol: I.

1-7-8-7-15

Army Form C. 2118.

B/73rd Brigade
R.F.A.
(New Army)

WAR DIARY
or
INTELLIGENCE SUMMARY.

(Erase heading not required.)

Place	Date	Hour	Summary of Events and Information	Remarks and references to Appendices
BULFORD Bulford	July 7	10 p.m.	AMESBURY Entrained at Amesbury Station, two trains of a ½ battery on each train. Strength 4 Officers (Capt. R.C. FREER, 2 Lieuts. E.S. PEARSE, G. KEELING, F.R. JOLLEY) 132 other ranks, 129 horses.	
SOUTHAMPTON	8		Detrained at 3 a.m. Embarked 6 a.m. Sailed 4 p.m.	
LE HAVRE	9		Disembarked 8 a.m. Entrained on one train 12 midnight.	
ST OMER	11		Detrained 1 a.m. Marched to BONNINGUES. Remainder time in billets during concentration of the division. Thence the artillery of the division marched to LAPUGNOY (3 marches), and remained there in reserve.	
	20		The LX (Lt. KEELING) went into action at CAMBRIN attached to 30th (Bath) R.F.A. On 24th LX returned to Bn. and was replaced by RX (Lt. JOLLEY).	
	27th		The LX moved up and took over a position at LES BREBIS from the 22nd London Battery, Wagon line at DROUVIN.	
	28th		The RX departed. All men were carried out at night. Clear moonlight. Registration carried out daily on a wide front from 90° to 130° true bearing	

Ranges from 3400ˣ to 4800ˣ. All observation had to be from right forwards in a line with our infantry trenches. Several days were taken over registration, as it was desired to give only a few rounds daily so as not to give information of arrival of new batteries.

121/6754

15th Known

73rd Bde: RFA.
Vol: II
August 15.

WAR DIARY
or
INTELLIGENCE SUMMARY.

Place	Date	Hour	Summary of Events and Information	Remarks and references to Appendices
LE BREBIS	2/8/15	-	"D" Battery took up Position & commenced to Register	
-	3/8/15	-	Brigade staff moved by Road to NOEUX-LES-MINES as Reinf. Group. O.C Brigade assumed command of Reserve Group which consisted of A/173, B/70, C/71, D/72. In addition to these Batteries, took command of all Wagon lines of Divisional Arty.	
NOEUX-LES-MINES	7.8.15	9am	A/Bty 73rd Brigade marched by Road to LOCRE a two days march. And was attached to 28th Division.	
	17th		B/70 Relieved A/70 in action.	
	18th		C/71 Relieved A/71 in action	
	19th		D/72 Relieved A/72 in action	
	20th		Marched to MAZINGARBE. & Prepared to take over batteries of 73rd Bde in action	

G. W. Whiteing Lt. Col.

121/6874

15th Division

13/73 Battery
Vol II

August 15

Army Form C. 2118.

WAR DIARY
or
INTELLIGENCE SUMMARY.
(Erase heading not required.)

72nd Bde RFA
No. 73/13

Place	Date	Hour	Summary of Events and Information	Remarks and references to Appendices
LES BREBIS	August 1st to 4th		Continued Registration. Battery now forms part of W group, with 3 18pdr batteries under Col. STIRLING.	
	5th	7.0 p.m.	Fired 60 rounds HE onto a point of front line trench which appeared to have been much strengthened recently. Also batteries 72nd Bde USA rd also fired shrapnel.	
		6 p.m.	Fired 20 rounds HE onto SNIPERS POST at S. end of PUITS 16. Scored two direct hits. Then fired two rounds on PUITS 16, all of which were effective on the houses and building.	
	7th	6 p.m.	Fired 40 rounds HE on observation post in front of DOUBLE CRASSIER. Several went blind as they pitched just over and slid down the further slope, and at first we were heard to rochet and burst on record impact. The observation post was eventually damaged by two direct hits and a communication trench destroyed.	
	10th		Battery reduced to cover only W1 and W2; it is very dangerous over to the troops on our right and even a rise to the hayrick of French Battery on our right is so to communicate over then	

WAR DIARY
or
INTELLIGENCE SUMMARY.
(Erase heading not required.)

Army Form C. 2118.

Place	Date	Hour	Summary of Events and Information	Remarks and references to Appendices
August	27	2 p.m.	Registration was completed by 16th. After this we only fired occasionally, mostly in retaliation when the enemy shelled out trenches and billets. Instead of firing merely a salvo then wait 5 minutes before firing again, we fired 55 rounds HE or two rounds G.F. about short range. Operation being carried out by everyone. The Mortar worked direct with an Obs. Post with Target.	
	28		Started to prepare a new position about 1½ miles S. of VERMELLES. Zone to be covered from VERMELLES – HULLOCH road to a little S. of VERMELLES–LENS road, a front of 80°. Were carried on by day & night so only a few men could be spared from the guns at a time.	

R.H. Stuckey Capt R.V.A.

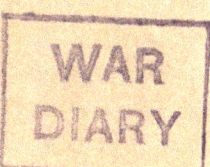

Headquarters,

73rd BRIGADE, R.F.A.

(15th Division)

S E P T E M B E R

1 9 1 5

Army Form C. 2118.

WAR DIARY
or
INTELLIGENCE SUMMARY.
(Erase heading not required.)

September 1915

Instructions regarding War Diaries and Intelligence Summaries are contained in F. S. Regs., Part II. and the Staff Manual respectively. Title pages will be prepared in manuscript.

Place	Date	Hour	Summary of Events and Information	Remarks and references to Appendices
MAZINGARBE	2nd		Grouped with O.C. 90th Bde R.F.A.	Attach'n
	3rd		Took over control of B/73. for Lateral Purposes, from 72nd Bde R.F.A.	#1
	4th		Enemy Shelled our trenches C. Battery retaliated G.35.a.6.3	#2
	5th		Nothing to Report	#3
	6th		Grouped under O.C. 13th Bde for Lateral Purposes	#4
	7th		Section of 17th London Battery R.F.A. attached to us	#5
	8th		Nothing to Report	#6
	9th		Enemy Shelled our Infantry on LENS road C Battery retaliated G.34. C.77. + G.38.c.91	#7
	10th		Nothing to Report	#8
	11th		"	#9
	12th		"	#10
	13th	11.15am	1 Gun C/73 Burst when firing Shot yL killing Sgt L. + wounding Sgt Knott, Cpl Taylor, L. Weedman, Gr Pitt	#11
			Nothing to Report — Registered Points by Aeroplane	#12
	14th		Registered several Points by Aeroplane	#13
	15th			#14

Army Form C. 2118

WAR DIARY
or
INTELLIGENCE SUMMARY.
(Erase heading not required.)

Instructions regarding War Diaries and Intelligence Summaries are contained in F. S. Regs., Part II. and the Staff Manual respectively. Title pages will be prepared in manuscript.

Place	Date	Hour	Summary of Events and Information	Remarks and references to Appendices
	16th			
	17th		Registered several Points by Aeroplane Observation in LOOS. HILL 70. Puits 14 Bis. & Communication Trenches.	AM 7
	18th			
	19th			
	20th			
	21st	6 am	Commenced Bombardment. 80 Rounds Per gun Per day allowed for Bombardment. Shelled Communication Trenches & other Points Registered.	AM 7
	22nd		Second Day of Bombardment. Carried out Programme. About 3 men were killed & two wounded in D/13. One man wounded & two men Transferred that night for Interference with guns - AM 7	AM 7
	23rd		Third Day of Bombardment. Carried out Programme. Thunderstorm about 7 pm. lasted about an hour.	AM 7
	24th		Fourth day of Bombardment. Rained during night of 23/24th. Rained at intervals during the day.	AM 7

1577 Wt. W10791/1773 500,000 1/15 D. D. & L. A.D.S.S./Forms/C. 2118.

WAR DIARY or INTELLIGENCE SUMMARY

Army Form C. 2118

September 1915

Place	Date	Hour	Summary of Events and Information	Remarks and references to Appendices
	25th	5.50am	Commenced attack. 1st Phase, – 40 minutes – Batteries shelled Communication Trenches in their rear. C/73 fired 76 Rounds of Gas Shell into LOOS.	
		6.30am	2nd Phase – 10 minutes – Shelled Communication Trenches	
		6.40am	3rd Phase – 25 minutes – "C" Battery shelled LOOS. "B" Battery shelled Road leading from LOOS to PUITS, 14, BIS. "D" Bty shelled PUITS 14 BIS	
		7.5	1st Phase Batteries fired on Hill 70.	
		10am	"C" Battery was ordered forward in close support of Infantry. The Battery marched through LOOS to the Pylons – hoping to take up a position on the Eastern side of the Slag Heap. Lt Dewey, who had been sent forward to observe reported that our infantry were retiring from Hill 70. Whereupon the Battery retired through LOOS and came into action about 8.00 x N.E. of QUALITY STREET. One man Killed & two Wounded. 10 Horses Killed	

Army Form C. 2118

WAR DIARY
or
INTELLIGENCE SUMMARY.
(Erase heading not required.)

September 1915

Place	Date	Hour	Summary of Events and Information	Remarks and references to Appendices
	26th	—	During night 25/26th "B" & "C" Batteries moved forward to a position North of Loos and were subjected to Artillery, Rifle & Maxim fire which fortunately was directed too high. About 8.30 am Enemy counter-attacked. B & C Batteries having used up their ammunition retired abandoning Guns. The guns were recovered on the night of 26/27th and Brought into action at Fosse 7. One man killed four wounded. Three horses killed	
27th			Shelled Hill 70. Cite St Auguste and Puits 14 Bis as ordered. One man wounded	M/4 M/4
28th			Did not do much firing till 2.45 when Div: Arty: ordered heavy fire on Bois Hugo. All three batteries fired at rapid Rate till 3 Pm, when infantry attacked	M/4 M/4
29th			Did not fire	

WAR DIARY
INTELLIGENCE SUMMARY.

Army Form C. 2118

September 1915

(Erase heading not required.)

Instructions regarding War Diaries and Intelligence Summaries are contained in F. S. Regs., Part II. and the Staff Manual respectively. Title pages will be prepared in manuscript.

Place	Date	Hour	Summary of Events and Information	Remarks and references to Appendices
	30th		Did not fire	
			G.N.Mickem? Lt.Col R?A Comdg 93rd Bde R?A	

1/1/15

12/7432

15th Kurram

73rd Bde: R.F.A.
Vol: 4
Oct 15

WAR DIARY
or
INTELLIGENCE SUMMARY.

(Erase heading not required.)

Army Form C. 2118

43rd Bde RFA

October 1915

Place	Date	Hour	Summary of Events and Information	Remarks and references to Appendices
MAZINGARBE	1st	1.30 P.m	Fired 4 Rounds Per Battery on Railway in N1 C.I.8.	9117
	2nd		CITE ST LAURENT. Registered several points between Puits 14 Bis & CITE ST LAURENT.	9117
	3rd		CITE ST ELIE. Registered Wood in H26, and Enemy Line of Trenches through H20, H26 d, to Hood H29 a. Fired on Road through H7 C & a. to North of CITE ST ELIE from 5.30 P.m to 6.30 P.m.	9117
	4th		Endeavoured to Register several points by Aeroplane observation but failed. Nothing special to Report.	9117
	5th		Again tried to Register by Aeroplane but failed. Nothing to Report.	9117
	6th		Registered Puits 13 Bis.	9117
	7th		Registered Trenches in front of points in AUCHY CH	9117
	8th		Enemy attacked in Region of Chalk Pit Wood about 4.25 P.m. The attack lasted till about 8 P.m. Brigade fired on HULLUCH PUITS 14 Bis, Hoods in H26 & H27. Enemy fired a large number of rounds in old Front line Trenches. The gas	9117

WAR DIARY
or
INTELLIGENCE SUMMARY.
(Erase heading not required.)

Army Form C. 2118

Place	Date	Hour	Summary of Events and Information	Remarks and references to Appendices
	8th		Continued:- Made thy gyro water, but did no further damage.	A/117
	9th		Stroke of the Nicking. Returned to England. Major C. St. M. Ingham took over Command (Brigade) Nothing to Report.	A/117
	10th		Registered points in Hulluch & trenches in front of Hulluch. Also Registered Points on Road in H.6. Fired on Railway south of Puits 14 Bis also Enemy trench east of Chalk Pit Wood	A/117
	11th		Continued Registration in Region of Hulluch	A/117
	12th		Nothing to Report	A/117
	13th	12.50 pm	Fired in support of Infantry attack as follows:- Trenches in front of Hulluch for 30 min. fired 600 Rds HE On houses on both sides of Road on S.W. face of Hulluch for 40 min fired 300 Rds HE (One Bty) One Bty on Trench in front of Hulluch, from H 19 a 8.3 to H 19 a 6.6. One Bty on trench at Hulluch from H 13 a 2.5 to H 13 a 9.3	A/117
		1.20 pm	Each Battery fired 360 Rds HE (40 min)	

WAR DIARY
or
INTELLIGENCE SUMMARY.

Army Form C. 2118

October 1915

Place	Date	Hour	Summary of Events and Information	Remarks and references to Appendices
	13th	2 Pm	All Batteries fired on Houses both sides of Road N & W face of HULLUCH from H.13 d.2.5 to H.13 d.2.2. Fired 420 Rds H.E. (80 min)	
		2.30 Pm	Formed a Barrage in HULLUCH H.13 d.4.3 to H.13 d.7.0 fired 300 Rds H.E. (30 min)	
		3 Pm	Formed a Barrage in HULLUCH, H.13 d.7.0 to H.13 d.1.7 fired 240 Rds (30 min)	
		3.30 Pm	Fired till 6 Pm on last Barrage one Rd per gun every three minutes	
		8 Pm	"D" Bty fired on Trench H.19 d.5.4 & d.7.2, 10 Rds per hour till 6 am	
		8.45 Pm	C Bty fired on H.14 C.8.3 10 Rds per hour till 6 am Did not fire	
	14th		Did not fire	AM7
	15th		Nothing to Report	AM7
	16th		Registered Trench in front of HULLUCH	AM7
	17th			AM7

Army Form C. 2118

WAR DIARY
or
INTELLIGENCE SUMMARY.
(Erase heading not required.)

October 1915

Instructions regarding War Diaries and Intelligence Summaries are contained in F. S. Regs., Part II. and the Staff Manual respectively. Title pages will be prepared in manuscript.

Place	Date	Hour	Summary of Events and Information	Remarks and references to Appendices
	18th	1 Pm	Concentrated on Northern Half of BOIS HUGO. Fired 6 Rds per gun as fast as guns could be laid carefully.	9/11/7
		1.10 Pm	Fired 4 more Rounds per gun on Same Place. Result of fire not known	
	19th	3 Pm	Fired 8 Rds per gun from all Batteries on H14 C 44 to H13 D 9.1	
		4 Pm	Concentrated on German Front Line trench from H13 a 4 2 to H13 a 2.6. Fired 10 Rds per gun. Ceased fire at 4.20 R. Result of firing not known.	9/11/7
	20th		Section of Each Bty. moved to VERMELLES, into Action. Nothing Special to Report	9/11/7
	21st		Registered several guns in CITE ST ELIE & trenches west of it.	9/11/7
	22d		On Bg Lt 21-22 Remands of R.A. moved into action at VERMELLES. Registered as on 21st	7/11/7
	23d		Concentrated fire on CITE ST ELIE at 11 am & 11.20 am fired about 96 Rds.	9/11/7

WAR DIARY or INTELLIGENCE SUMMARY.

Army Form C. 2118

October 1915

Date	Hour	Summary of Events and Information	Remarks and references to Appendices
24th 25th		Continued Registration. Nothing Special. Report awaited. D/73 fired 4 Rds on Quarries every 2 hrs to prevent working. C/73rd fired H.E.1.1. 16 L.8.3. to Counter Bty. Engage batteries at H.E.1.1. 16 L.8.3.	AHH AHH
26th		D/73 fired on Quarries throughout the day, 4 Rds every 2 hours. Registered several points in CITE ST ELIE	AHH
27th		Registered Points in CITE ST ELIE. Fired on Quarries as on Dec 25th & 26th. At 3 am, East Bty fired 20 Rds H.E. B'yc 13 Bty on HULLUCH, D Bty on CITE ST ELIE. Repeated at 5 am	AHH
28th		Continued Registration. Fired on Quarries as on 27th	AHH AHH
29th		Continued Registration. 1 neg Gm G narres rom 28 L One B'ty (B) ordered by 15th D.A. to fire 4 Rds every two hours on trench y5d hull East. Registered. Fired on Quarries.	AHH AHH
30th		Registered CITE ST ELIE & Quarries & Trench in front of CITE	AHH AHH

Army Form C. 2118

WAR DIARY
or
INTELLIGENCE SUMMARY.
(Erase heading not required.)

Oct 1915

Place	Date	Hour	Summary of Events and Information	Remarks and references to Appendices
	30th		ST. ELIE at 1 am. (7 rnds 120 Rds) fired on enemies trench as on 30th. Concentrated on HULLUCH at 2.30 am & again at 5.15 am & fired 72 Rds on each occasion	A/117
	31st			A/117

Wylierin Major
o.nd of 73rd 134th Bty 8th

1577 Wt. W10791/1773 500,000 1/15 D.D. & L. A.D.S.S./Forms/C. 2118.

43rd Bde: RFA.
Vol. 5

121/7678

15th Hussars

Nov 15.

WAR DIARY / INTELLIGENCE SUMMARY

Army Form C. 2118.

Bde R.F.A. November 1915

Place	Date	Hour	Summary of Events and Information	Remarks and references to Appendices
VERMELLES	1st		Fired 4 Rds every 2 Hours during day on Quarries also 4 Rds twice during night. Fired 4 Rds every two Hours on trench in G 5 d. 4 of the 4th in support	#114
	2nd		Fired on Quarries & trench in G 5 d. so on F" #114 fired on HULLUCH WINDLES at 6 am	#114
	3rd		72 Rds fired. Fired on QUARRIES & TRENCH in G 5 L noon & nothing further to R/ of Bty	#114
	4th		Concentrated on Fosse Alley at 11.5 am 11.55 am fired 144 Rds H.E.	#114
	5th		Concentrated on CITÉ ST ELIE at 12.20 P.m & 4.30p.m. 72 Rds each time. Concentrated on Fosse Alley at 1.50 P.m. fired 72 Rds. Gun of 13/13 injured by premature. Had to be returned to Rlwhead	#114
	6th		Concentrated on ST ELIE at 5 Pm	#114
	7th		Concentrated on ST ELIE at 1 am fired 144 Rds.	#114
	8th		Concentrated on ST ELIE at 3.10 Pm & 11.5 Pm 208 Rds. Demolished Watertower at Puits 13.	#114

Army Form C. 2118.

WAR DIARY
or
INTELLIGENCE SUMMARY.
(Erase heading not required.)

B for 4 Nov 1915

Place	Date	Hour	Summary of Events and Information	Remarks and references to Appendices
	9th		Nothing Special to Report.	9/11/4
	10th		Concentrated on ST ELIE from 11.45 am to 12.45 pm fired 120 Rds. The Battery of W.B/73 was hit by 8" Armour Piercing. This is the third time the house has been hit each time from a different direction. Nothing Special to Report. One man slightly wounded on 10th Remained at duty.	9/11/4
	11th		Fired 144 Rds HE at Quarries during day. Concentrated at 12.30 pm on Junction in front of ST ELIE.	10/11/4 9/11/4
	12th		Nothing to Report	9/11/4
	13th		Concentrated on Junction in front of ST ELIE.	9/11/4
	14th		C/73 attacked to O.C 3rd Bgde R.F.A. for Fire Purposes.	
	15th		A 9" H.E hit one of the Gun Pits of C/73 wounding a Sergeant. The hit was an ascending the enemy are keeping up a fairly steady slow 200 yds in front of C/73. Sgt Major S/73 wounded — Died in Hospital	9/11/4

WAR DIARY or INTELLIGENCE SUMMARY

Army Form C. 2118

73rd Bde R.F.A. Nov 1915

Place	Date	Hour	Summary of Events and Information	Remarks and references to Appendices
	16th		Fired during day on Enemy Front Line & Support Lines. Nothing Special to Report	
	17th		Nothing Special to Report	
	18th		1 P.M. Concentration on ST ELIE. Nothing to Report	
	19th			
	20th			
	21st		11.30 a.m. Concentrated on ST ELIE. 2.40 Concentrated on ST ELIE. B. Bty fired at a "nomad" in front of St Elie. Hit it 10 times. The enemy drew up incalculties of timber. Firing at this moment seemed to annoy the German. Nothing Special to Report	
	22nd		Nothing Special to Report	
	23rd		2/13 howitzer Bty VERMELLES, C. a position near ANNEQUIN. Trench lit to fire on HOHENZOLLERN REDOUBT	
	24th		C. Bty Billett hit by a High Velocity 5.9 - 5.9s are nearby. Showers of high velocity nothing special to Report	
	25th		Nothing Special to Report	

WAR DIARY
or
INTELLIGENCE SUMMARY.

Army Form C. 2118

Oct 1915

Place	Date	Hour	Summary of Events and Information	Remarks and references to Appendices
	26th		Nothing Special to Report. Snowed heavily 12.30p.m to 11p	
	27th		Had a 4 nightmen at 12 noon & 7pm a strong SE	
			three of wind. Nothing to report	
	28th		Nothing Special to Report	
	29th		The enemy fired a few minenwerfer shells some then several	
			we retaliated successfully.	
	30th		Nothing Special to Report	

R C Desbabès
Major RFA
Comdg 13 S Bde RFA

1/11/15

73 afore RTa.
vol. 6

798/1

15th Rin

Army Form C. 2118.

73rd Bde R.H.A

WAR DIARY
or
INTELLIGENCE SUMMARY.
(Erase heading not required.)

73 Bde R.H.A December 1915

Place	Date	Hour	Summary of Events and Information	Remarks and references to Appendices
	1st		Nothing Special to Report. Fired at & damaged cross trench. Retaliated for German shelling. Nothing further to report	Attack
	2nd		Met a German working party in Cross Alley	8417
	3rd		Nothing Special to Report	9117
	4th		Nothing Special to Report. (Gale blowing)	F.H.C.
	5th		Heavy Shelling on the whole of our front by Enemy in retaliation for our strafe on the Dwarsiek.	F.H.C.
	6th		Nothing Special to Report.	F.H.C.
	7th		Enemy shelled Vermelles. (we blew up a machine gun)	F.H.C.
	8th		We effectively strafed Bill's Bluff and the south most salient of the 9 tents.	F.H.C
	9th		We blew up a Bomb Store in Enemy trench running to Pt 45 from the Dwarsiek, causing much debris to fall in our lines, including portions of Germans & a dog.	F.H.C.
	10		Shelled two strong pits effectively	F.H.C.

WAR DIARY
or
INTELLIGENCE SUMMARY.
(Erase heading not required.)

Army Form C. 2118.

Place: 43rd Bde R.F.A.
December 1915

Date	Hour	Summary of Events and Information	Remarks and references to Appendices
11th		Intermittent shelling. Our guns started a conflagration in the neighbourhood of Loos & the Loos which gave off dense volumes of smoke for 24 hours. Nothing special to report.	7. H. C.
12th		Sent 2 Representations to Auchel to take our billets from 6" London B=	7. H. C.
13		Heavy shelling on both sides in our sector. Nothing special to Report.	7. H. C.
14		B- D' B'ds + Am= Col. moved with H'd Qrs to Auchel + took over billets from 6" London Brigade 47' Div=. C Bats remaining in action with 1 subsection of B.A.C.	7. H. C. 7. H. C. 7. H. C.
15			
16th		Nothing to Report	
17th		Nothing to Report	
18th		Nothing to Report.	
19th		Arranged details of training for the week.	7. H. C.
20		Signaller Class started. + Gunnery Instruction Class for (Officers)	
21st		Artillery Special to Report.	7. H. C.

WAR DIARY
or
INTELLIGENCE SUMMARY.

Army Form C. 2118

73rd Bde R.F.A.   December 1915

Place	Date	Hour	Summary of Events and Information	Remarks and references to Appendices
Auchel	22		Instruction Classes continued	H.H.C.
	23		Arrangements made to give the Troops a Special Dinner on Xmas Day.	H.H.C.
	24		Nothing Special to Report	
	25		Christmas Day.	
	26		Received Order for C.B.5 to come out of action & proceed to Auchel. One Section to move out on the nights of 27th & 28th	H.H.C.
	27		One Section of C.B.5 - half section of B.A.C arrived at Auchel & were billeted in Rue de Milieu.	H.H.C.
	28		The above Section of C.B.5 & B.A.C. went back to Vermelles & took up their old positions in Action.	H.H.C.
	29		A new Padre Capt. Churchill attached to 73rd B.de & posted to B.de Amm. Col. Mess	H.H.C.
	30		Received instructions from D.A. for one Battery to hold itself in readiness to return to Action. Schyn	H.H.C.
	31		Sent billeting Parties to Westrehem for selection of billets.	H.H.C.

W H Anderson
Lieut Col
Comdt 73rd Bde R.F.A

C O N F I D E N T I A L.

War Diary

of

73rd Brigade Royal Field Arty

From 1st September, 1916 to 30th September, 1916.

Volume Number 15

[signature]

Major, R.A.

Bde Major 15th Divisional Arty.

73.Bde. R.A.
Vol: 7

15

WAR DIARY or INTELLIGENCE SUMMARY

43rd Bde R.F.A. January 1916

Place	Date	Hour	Summary of Events and Information	Remarks
Auchel	1st		Nothing Special to report - Church Parade.	
	2nd		Nothing Special to report.	
	3rd		Nothing Special to Report	
	4th		Divisional Parade.	
	5th		Bde. and marched via CAUCHY-a-la-TOUR - AMES - LIERES - AVEHY-au-BOIS - LIGNY-lez-AIRE - GUHEM to ENGUIN-les-MINES where Brigade Billetted for the night. 5/16	
	6th		Marched to DELETTE and Reconnoitred Positions for Batteries in the line DIHEM - MAISNIL at DELETTE. Orders to return were issued & Brigade Returned to ENGUIN-les-MINES where billets were taken for night 6/7"	
	7th		Marched to AUCHEL to Near Billetts via GUHEM - LIGNY-lez- AIRE - AVCHY au BOIS - FERFAY. On Section 1 B/73, moved into action with 4/4 Div. B/73 did not accompany Brigade on the march	

WAR DIARY
or
INTELLIGENCE SUMMARY.
(Erase heading not required.)

73rd Bde R.F.A.

January 1916

Place	Date	Hour	Summary of Events and Information	Remarks and references to Appendices
AVEHEL	8th		Remaining Section of B/73 moved into Action with 41st Div: We now have two Batteries, D/73 and B/73 in action with 41st Div.	Attached
	9th		Nothing to Report.	Attached
	10th		Inspected by Major Genl F.W.McCRACKEN, Cmdg 15th Division	F.H.Q
	11th		Nothing Special to report	F.H.Q
	12th & 13th		Arrangements made to move back into Action on 16th & Wagon Lines selected at Mieux-les-Mines.	
	14th		Nothing to report	F.H.Q
	15th		Night of 15/16 one section of each Battery went into Action & 16 B & D Battery at LONE T. C. Battery at LES BREBIS.	F.H.Q / MaRoc
	16		Brigade H.Q. Quarters moved to LES BREBIS, O.C. remaining Sections of Batteries moved into Action & Line Brigade took over responsibility for Line at 5.15 P.M.	F.H.Q

WAR DIARY
INTELLIGENCE SUMMARY

Army Form C. 2118.

73rd Bde R.F.A.

January 1916

Place	Date	Hour	Summary of Events and Information	Remarks and references to Appendices
LES BREBIS.	17		Nothing to Report	Y & C.
	18		Registration	
	19		"	
	20		"	
	21		"	
	22		"	
	23		Very satisfactory registration by aeroplane.	
	24		"	
	25		Nothing to report.	
	26		"	
	27		Heavy shelling by the Germans all day, to which this Brigade retaliated vigorously. At 5 P.M. the Germans attacked on our centre, but had no sooner left their trenches when they were driven back with heavy loss by our artillery. Machine gun fire.	
	28.		Heavy shelling all day on both sides - the enemy flew up a mine on our left front.	

WAR DIARY
or
INTELLIGENCE SUMMARY.

73rd Brigade RFA January 1916

Place	Date	Hour	Summary of Events and Information	Remarks and references to Appendices
Les Brebis	29th January		Very quiet day, probably owing to heavy fog? Usual artillery activity. Nothing to report.	
	30th		"	
	31st		"	

Alyma Short
Commanding,
73rd Brigade R.F.A

Army Form C. 2118.

WAR DIARY
or
INTELLIGENCE SUMMARY.

73rd Brigade RFA   February 1916.

Place	Date	Hour	Summary of Events and Information	Remarks and references to Appendices
LES BREBIS	1st Feb.		Severe artillery activity on both sides. Several new caps revealed by air photographs. This Brigade ordered to demolish them.	97!
	2nd Feb.		Artillery still very active.	97!
	3rd Feb.		Very heavy shelling by the enemy, especially in the LOOS sector, to which this Brigade retaliated. Aeroplanes very active.	97!
	4th Feb.		Continued artillery activity. Exceptional railway activity reported at WINGLES.	97!
	5th Feb.		Very heavy shelling, especially in LOOS sector. Railway activity still above normal at WINGLES. Frightfulness no. 264.	97!
	6th Feb.		G. comparatively quiet day.	97!
	7th Feb.		Enemy bombarded Chalk Pit & trenches north & south of it, to which we retaliated.	97!
	8th		Nothing special to report.	97!
	9th		C Battery shelled with gas shells, necessitating use of gas helmets. Heavy shelling on both sides.	97!

Army Form C. 2118.

DIARY
or
INTELLIGENCE SUMMARY.

(Erase heading not required.)

73d Brigade RFA   February 1916.

Place	Date	Hour	Summary of Events and Information	Remarks and references to Appendices
LES BREBIS	10th		Enemy shelled LOOS to which we retaliated. Nothing special to report. "Gas Alert".	App.
	11th		Have heavy shelling from trenches in LOOS section, to which we retaliated all day.	App.
	12th		Nothing to report. Enemy aeroplanes very active.	App.
	13th		Nothing to report. Owing to heavy wind.	App.
	14th		Destroyed an enemy H.Q. opposite LOOS	App.
	15th		Heavy gale blowing from S.W. Artillery quiet	App.
	16th		Gale continues. Corps Cmdr & CRA inspect battery positions.	App.
	17th		B Battery ordered to fire 3 quick salvos on road	App.
	18th		running through St ELIE 6.45 AM. Fired 13 shelled by us, but only 10 out of 30 rounds gave good bursts. Otherwise a very quiet day.	App.
	19th		Registration by aeroplane which had to be abandoned owing to extremely windy weather & bad light.	App.
	20th		Nothing special to report. B Battery ordered to fire 3 salvos on road running from N to S through St ELIE 7 AM.	App.

Army Form C. 2118.

WAR DIARY
or
INTELLIGENCE SUMMARY.

(Erase heading not required.)

Place: LES BREBIS
73d Bde RSA
February 15, 16.

Date	Hour	Summary of Events and Information	Remarks and references to Appendices
21st		B & D Batteries under heavy shell fire all day. No casualties.	M
22d		Quiet day owing to bad light & snow. D Battery caught a working party in the open, with good results	M.
23d		Heavy snow fall which prevented observation. A quiet day	M.
24th		Snow continues. Very little firing for fear of giving gun positions away.	M.
25th		Another quiet day. This Brigade ordered to stand by at 10 pm, as two mines were to be blown up in our area	M.
26th		Snow still on the ground. Very little firing	M.
27th		Snow still on the ground, but gradually thawing. Very quiet day.	M.
28th		Tried to register by aeroplane, but had to stop owing to bad light. Hostile aircraft very active. Demolished minenwerfer with 70th Bde 4 pm.	M.
29th		Fine day - Artillery & aircraft active. H.V. gun has two shoots, most of the shell falling into the trench	M.

[signature]
Lieut Col RSA

73 R.7.A.
Vol 9

WAR DIARY or INTELLIGENCE SUMMARY

Army Form C. 2118.

73rd Brigade R.F.A.   March 1916.

Place	Date	Hour	Summary of Events and Information	Remarks and references to Appendices
LES BREBIS	1st		Nothing to report. Aeroplane registration 2 rounds on H.9 at H32 c 54.	/17
	2nd		Nothing to report.	/17
	3rd		Rain and bad light prevented much artillery work. The brigade shelled H.Q.s rounds all day.	/17
	4th		On H.Q. at H15c76 with very good results. Fired 70 rounds of Active battery fire. Snowstorm prevented artillery work. This brigade fired on many different moments & H.Q.s with good results. Enemy working party in W30.	/17
	5th		Shelled Puits 14 bis (H.Q.s). Head Qrs at H32 A & H 12x4s. 7 rounds on H14A in retaliation. 6 rds on H13 d 36. 8 rounds on H20 b 64 (strong pt) 13 rds on H13 f 67 (O.P.) 30 rds on Fourth at H20 a 20 in retaliation. On the whole the detonations were very bad, owing to thaw.	/17
	6th		9 rounds on H14a. 12 rds on H14b. 38 rds on H20. 40 rds on H20 a 25 in retaliation 13 rds on H3axx, as hostile were seen at Chapel. Fouilakeul showing nearly the whole day. We shelled French on H19 b 95 ½ in retaliation.	/17
	7th		16 rounds on H13d in retaliation. 30 rounds on Chateau at H14 c 14, which is a suspected hostile O.P. 6 rounds on hostile wound at H30 b 65 obtaining two direct hits. 11 rounds on trench junction at H13 d 30. The ammunition in this last shoot was very poor – 7 rounds being blind, & 3 how hang fires etc.	/17
	8th			/17

Army Form C. 2118.

WAR DIARY
or
INTELLIGENCE SUMMARY.

(Erase heading not required.)

73a Brigade R.F.A.   March 1916.

Place	Date	Hour	Summary of Events and Information	Remarks and references to Appendices
LES BREBIS.	9th		Fired 10 rounds on H13d 2.6. 30 rounds on small quarry at H13a. 6 rounds on House in H14 b 3 D. 46 rounds at house at H15 a 7.6.	/A/.
	10th		Very quiet day owing to bad light. Fired 3 rounds H.E. on trench junction at H20 b 2.9. — one direct hit being obtained.	/A/. /A/.
	11th		20 rounds H.E. on H14 b and 24 rounds on H14 c in retaliation. Dull day.	
	12th		30 rounds on H13 a H1-7.5. 10 rds on H25 b 70. 15 rds on H13 b. 28 rounds on G13 d & H14 a. 30 rounds on trench junctions at G20 a 0.5, G20 b 3.9. and G20 b 6.5.4. 12 rounds on trench junction at G20 a 0.5. which did 46 rounds on Machine Gun emplacement at H31 b 1.5.2.4. 30 rounds on Cupola at H20 a 9.9. Material thrown into the air, but observing officer could not estimate the damage.	/A/.
	13th		2 rounds on H13 c 6.3. 6 rounds on H25 b 8.2. Hostile aircraft stopped further shelling. 6 rounds on H27 c H.9 & 3 rounds on H33 c 16 5 registration by aeroplane. Gunners on trench at H20 a 7.5 in retaliation 10 rounds of P at H20 b 6.5. 3 rounds on working party which dispersed them into the trench at H20 a IV. Results of fire could not be observed.	/A/.

1577 Wt.W10791/1773 500,000 1/15 D. D. & L. A.D.S.S./Forms/C. 2118.

WAR DIARY or INTELLIGENCE SUMMARY

Army Form C. 2118.

73rd Brigade R.F.A.   March 1916

Place	Date	Hour	Summary of Events and Information	Remarks and references to Appendices
LES BREBIS	14th		10 rds on H.13.d.3.6. 9 rds on N.2.a.5.30. Hits registration. 15 rounds on H.14.c.14 (Chateau) in retaliation. 4 rounds on Working Party at H.31.c.45. 6 rounds on rest working at H.30.c.2.3.7.4. in retaliation for enemy shelling FOSSE 7. 13 minutes or trench junction at H.30.b.64. 4 rounds at H.30.b.65" in retaliation.	
	15th		10 rds on H.13.d. 7 rds on C.T. ST EMILE 19 rds on O.P. at H.30.b.6.6" in retaliation. 13 rds on H.25.a.3 & H.31.b.1.6, movement seen. The enemy were observed working in the open throughout the day. Zeppelin was seen flying east- our FOSSE 7 at 10.45 pm.	9⁋7.
	16th		19 rounds on Quarry in H.13.a, but only two good detonations obtained. 8 rounds on PUITS 14 Bis (registration). Fired 9 rounds on enemy working party on H.31.d.60, which made for a dugout. 3 rounds on N.3.a.5.50, aeroplane registration. 19 rounds on trenches at H.25.d in retaliation for enemy shelling our front line in H.25.e and H.31.a heavily with 4.2's, 4.6.9 HE. 30% of our shell were blind. Shell parties were seen walking about the whole day. A carriage & pair was seen at H.3.a.	9⁋7.

WAR DIARY
INTELLIGENCE SUMMARY

73rd Brigade RGA month 9/16

Army Form C. 2118.

Place	Date	Hour	Summary of Events and Information	Remarks and references to Appendices
LES BREBIS.	17th		Intermittent shelling & retaliation the whole morning. At 10:45 AM in conjunction with the 70th Bde RGA, the HR Gun (in CHALK PIT) fired 20 rounds. 14 of which landed in the trench. Good detonations were obtained & a quantity of material was sent to fly up into the air.	
	18th		Working party observed at N15 D 3.9. 14 rounds fired in retaliation & observed to be observed for them. They did not wait to see more than one salvo owing to shortage of ammunition.	
	19th		10 rds on road in H15 B.O.4. 10 rds on working party at N1.B.0.4. Aeroplane over Wingles seen dropping white lights.	
	20th		9 rds on H20 A 4.9 in retaliation for enemy shelling G 24 with 4.2 HE. 19 rds in H 20 B 6.5. (OP) working party seen moving up at H 20 6 5.7 and at H 20 6 7.i.25.	
	21st		14 rds on French H30 b 4.6 in retaliation for enemy shelling G 24 with H 146 76. Shots seen opening from this house. 7208 Prospecto NE. 13 rds on house H146 76. Shots seen opening from this house. 19 rds in H 26 c. 16. in retaliation	
			On H25 D 34 H31 6 5.6. Checking line & registration of enemy shelling our front line in H2FG.	

Army Form C. 2118.

WAR DIARY
or
INTELLIGENCE SUMMARY.
(Erase heading not required.)

73rd Brigade RFA   March 1916

Place	Date	Hour	Summary of Events and Information	Remarks and references to Appendices
LES BREBIS	22.		10 rds on H.14.a and H.13.d in retaliation for enemy shelling H.19. Weather Dull.	
	23.		6 rounds on H.20.b.6.5. between men seen moving in trench.	
	24th		Test-attack at 10.31 A.M. very good results. Otherwise a very quiet day.	M1.
	25th		10 rounds on H.26.d in retaliation for enemy shelling H.25.c. +rds in retaliation on H.20.b.65. 6 rds on working party. Putting up wire at H.13.d.70, which dispersed them probably killing several men. Four trains seen near WINGLES. 10 rds H.E on H.13.d.2.6 to check error of the day for a probable important night shoot.	J Mullett
	26th		A very quiet day. Orderly Officer of 97th Bde RFA attaches for 4 days for instruction.	
	27th		6 rds on trench in H.20.a in retaliation for enemy shelling G.34.b. 6 rds H.E on working party at N.1.b.04. This caused casualties & drove up a lot of material. Work erected. Flashes of a battery in action seen 25 RT at VENDIN CHURCH point. at 4 pm. N.R. gun shot 15 rds, 10 landing in trench. At 4.45 PM fired 10 rds, 7 in trench. 1500 HQ. Killed with 5.9 HE he casualties. 11 trains seen at MEURCHIN.	M1

1577 Wt. W10791/4773 500,000 1/15 D. D. & L. A.D.S.S./Forms/C. 2118.

WAR DIARY
or
INTELLIGENCE SUMMARY

Army Form C. 2118.

73rd Bde R.F.A.   March 1916.

Place	Date	Hour	Summary of Events and Information	Remarks and references to Appendices
LES BREBIS	28th		Fired 40 rounds NE on H.13a.3+7/9 where guessed gun was bombing attack in that sector. Also 5 rounds on H.13a.5.1. 5 H.E. on N.13.04. dispersing working party. 5 H.E. on H.25.0 in retaliation for enemy shelling an aeroplane 5 on 930d. 4 gun shell was being fired near approaching from PONT A VENDIN in a N.E. direction. Seen proceeding from METALLURGIQUE to MEURCHIN, also from MEUCHIN to METALLURGIQUE.	#7
	29th		5.5 HE on H.13.06.1/54 H.13.075 to H.13a dragoon of infantry which appeared to have the effect of dispersing mowing enemy. 10 rounds on communication trenches in that sector. Also HE at H.31.d.45 where however none seen. The Travis Cinema men WINGES during the day. CHALK PIT WOOD shelled with 5.9's between 12:35 pm—9.8 P.M. 2 rounds on small roof running along road at H.5.d.79. Both shell were blind, but the Huns were seen to lie down + then crawl over the sky line.	#7

WAR DIARY or INTELLIGENCE SUMMARY

73rd Bde R.F.A. March 1916

Army Form C. 2118.

Place	Date	Hour	Summary of Events and Information	Remarks and references to Appendices
Les Brebis	30.		A lot of movement was seen during the morning. G/123, our forward mine wagons, the crews of whose Arch'd Gun on bearing of 6630 h, of WINGLES WATER TOWER in H.10.d. fired Garages. 16 rounds on H.20.c.48.97730.? in retaliation for enemy shelling Q24.6 with 4.5" from VENDIN-LE-VIEIL. Movement seen. Hammelle Par-Movement seen. Enemy observation balloons got went up at METALURGIQUE. STAUGUST VILLENS. During the day, 5" trains were seen at CARVIN 9-11 at WINGLES	J.V.
	31.		9 rounds NE on working parties at H.31.d.60 H.31.d.65 NICOD wart carroul. 6HE on H.25.d.3.2. In retaliation. JHE 1.20575. in retaliation.	J.V.

H. Pugh Cap't R.F.A.
Comdg 73rd Bde R.F.A.

Vol 10

Army Form C. 2118.

1/73 RFA

WAR DIARY
or
INTELLIGENCE SUMMARY.
(Erase heading not required.)

73d Bde. RFA.   April 1916

Place	Date	Hour	Summary of Events and Information	Remarks and references to Appendices
LES BREBIS.	1		4 HE on H13, small enemy minnenwerf up, but everything was quiet. 30 HE on H13c 47½ to H13a 35 by order of 15 DA which seemed to have very good effect. 6HE on Trench in H30e in retaliation.	44
	2		4 HE H23a which quelled hostile bombing activity on that sector. 6 HE H26 c18 + 8 rounds in enemy front line in H30 c, in retaliation. Signs of Trench mortar seen at H30 d 738 + H19 d 732. Shots were put up in front of trench H279a,7-43.	44
	3		Too hazy for shooting — Very Quiet	
	4		2 Rds HE on H13a to locate enemy Bombing. 4 Pm to 6 Pm drafted occasional Rounds on enemy Strong line to annoy them. Sausage pit; Detached O.P. at H20 d 65 it was referred early light.	#117
	5		Started our second line from 4 Pm to 6.30 Pm about 25 Rds S.O.S. call at midnight 5½ fired 60 Rds on night lines, had another effective shoot at H 26 d 65	#117
	6		Enemy shelled H 19 a,c all day from 8 am to 4 Pm with H20 a + 5,9 we retaliated w[ith] /46 Rds	#117

Army Form C. 2118.

WAR DIARY or INTELLIGENCE SUMMARY.

(Erase heading not required.)

73rd By R.F.A.   April 1916

Place	Date	Hour	Summary of Events and Information	Remarks and references to Appendices
Sibuhr	7th		Worried the Second line during day, fired about 64 Rds. Enemy very quiet.	M.O.7
	8th		Quiet all day, about 9.17pm Enemy sprang a mine on R.T. of Divisional front. Batteries at once opened fire on hight fair, rather offered. Huttered. Then sent up a lot of Red Rockets. Probably in an endeavour to make us waste Amm. Very quiet.	M.O.7
	9th		Enemy fired a lot of 5.9o at Horse 7. did not do any harm to our Batteries	M.O.7 M.O.7
	10th			
	11th		Fired on several Working Parties & Defences then, 9 again got several hits on [P.at] 1130 & 95.	M.O.7
	12th		Very Quiet. Enemy had a few 4.2o into L.008 - Half Battery fired on a few Working Parties on Hill 70. Nothing further to report.	M.O.7 M.O.7
	13th			
	14th			M.

Army Form C. 2118.

WAR DIARY
or
INTELLIGENCE SUMMARY.
(Erase heading not required.)

73d Bde RFA April 1916

Place	Date	Hour	Summary of Events and Information	Remarks and references to Appendices
LES BREBIS.	15th		LES BREBIS Allotted with 4.5" & 5" guns. Observed nothing to report.	A.
	16th		Brigade Head Quarters & D Battery moved into rest at LIERES.	A.
	17th		Brigade Ammunition Column arrived at LIERES 11 AM.	A.
	18th		General Training & baths at BEUVRY.	A.
	19th			
	20th		5 places allotted to Officers of 73d Bde RFA to attend lecture at LILLERS by the 1st Army Intelligence Officer. One other rank sent on a signalling course at LIETTRES.	A.
	21st		nothing to report.	
	22d			
	23d		Brigade Inspection by Brig. General McCracken Brigade Competition for Best Section won by C/173.	
	24th		nothing to report.	
	25th			
	26th		C Battery and one section of the BAC ordered to reinforce the 16th Division	

Army Form C. 2118.

WAR DIARY
or
INTELLIGENCE SUMMARY.
(Erase heading not required.)

73rd Bde R.F.A.   April 1916

Place	Date	Hour	Summary of Events and Information	Remarks and references to Appendices
LIÈRES	27th		B/73, D/73, remainder of B.A.C. & B.d.H.Q. Stand to.	/ts.
	28th	12.30 p.m.	C/73 1 section B/73 + 1 section D/73 relieves 12th D.A. The Order to stand down received.	/ts.
LIÈRES & BETHUNE	29th		1 section B/73 + 1 section D/73 with remainder of B.A.C. relieves 12th D.A.	/ts.
BETHUNE	30th		73rd Bde H.Q. moved to Bethune. Nothing to report.	/ts.

Wippman
Commanding,
73rd Brigade R.F.A.

WAR DIARY

C/73" BRIGADE R.F.A.

30ᵗʰ April to
8ᵗʰ June.

1916.

Army Form C. 2118.

C/73 RFA
15 DIV.

Vol 1

WAR DIARY
or
INTELLIGENCE SUMMARY.
(Erase heading not required.)

Place	Date	Hour	Summary of Events and Information	Remarks and references to Appendices
Gibenchy	APRIL 30.		Very quiet day.	Number Rounds Fired per Day
				462. Bx
	MAY			
	1.		Fired on G5A in retaliation at 8.25 pm — at 2 pm fired on G5b, G5a.	27. 13x
	2.		Retaliation Obstructive. Fine day — 500 light.	33. Bx
	3.		Fired on G5A 2pm — A30c 2.45 — G4b 6.40 pm.	37. 13x
	4.		Fired on G5A, G5Fd. G4b 6.40 pm in retaliation.	54.
	5.		During the day enemy shelled our trenches frequently. We retaliated on G5b, G5c, G5e, G5a, Bog G4a	122.
	6.		In retaliation for enemy shelling we fired on G5a, G5c.3.9.	209.
	7.		Retaliated on G5a, G4b, + G5a.2.8.	26.
	8.		In retaliation fired in enemy trenches at G5a.9.6, G5t.3.6.	63.
	9.		Quiet day — two repetitive several trench junctions	54.
	10.		Unusually quiet day.	NIL
	11.		Battle of the "KINK" Enemy shelled heavily with 5g. 4.5" & heavy TMs. We fired on the following points G5a, G4b, G5c, G5a.2.8, G5t.2.4. – We lost two lines of trenches	1042.

Army Form C. 2118.

WAR DIARY
or
INTELLIGENCE SUMMARY.
(Erase heading not required.)

R.F.A
C/73. 15 DIV.

Instructions regarding War Diaries and Intelligence Summaries are contained in F. S. Regs., Part II. and the Staff Manual respectively. Title pages will be prepared in manuscript.

Place	Date	Hour	Summary of Events and Information	Remarks and references to Appendices
	MAY			Number of rounds fired per day
	12.		Bombarded G5d & G5c central - attempt to repair HERN & KINK failed	436 Bx.
	13.		Retaliatory Bombardment. Quiet day. We retaliate to enemy's fire.	37 "
	14.		We heavily strafes G5d central	609 "
	15.		Very quiet day -	NIL "
	16.		Fire on G5d in retaliation	18 "
	17.		Enemy shelled our trenches in G11 a+c, G4 & 10 squares, we retaliated on strong points	319 "
	18.		Quiet day -	NIL "
	19.		—do—	
	20.		Enemy fairly active with 4.2's & Minnie - we retaliated -	27 "
	21.		Enemy's minnie active - we fires on suspected Minnie emplacements	36 "
	22.		Our trenches (round HOHENZOLLERN REDOUBT and shelled - we fires on string points.	43 "
	23.		We retaliates on enemy trenches in G5c + d - G4b.	73 "
	24.		Our trenches in G4, 10 & 11 squares were heavily shelled - we fires at Trench junctions + silenced minnie at N.E. of DUMP.	157 "

Army Form C. 2118.

C/73 R.F.A.
15 Div

WAR DIARY
or
INTELLIGENCE SUMMARY.
(Erase heading not required.)

Instructions regarding War Diaries and Intelligence Summaries are contained in F. S. Regs., Part II. and the Staff Manual respectively. Title pages will be prepared in manuscript.

Place	Date	Hour	Summary of Events and Information	Remarks and references to Appendices
S of Authuille	MAY			Rounds fired per by
	25		Enemys artillery quiet. We registered several targets in G5 square.	24 13 x
	26		In retaliation for 5.9"s + 4.2"s on our trenches in G 10 + 11 squares throughout the day, we fired on strong points.	51
	27		Quiet day. We retaliated for Minnies.	16
	28		He fired on trench junction in G 4 + 5 squares. Enemy fairly quiet.	26
	29		In the early morning + in various stages the enemy in our outer zone - throughout the day retaliated for 5.9"s + 4.2"s	121
	30		Quiet day. We registered trench junction &c in G 5 b square.	16
	31		Very quiet -	6
	JUNE			
	1		In retaliation for enemys 4.2"s + 5.9"s we fired on strong points -	77
	2		He fires in retaliation for 4.2" on trench junction in G5 square.	38
	3		He fires on M.G emplacement in G5c square	11
	4		Retaliates on enemy trenches at G6d in retaliation for Minnies. We fired on his target during the day.	38

Army Form C. 2118.

WAR DIARY
or
INTELLIGENCE SUMMARY.
(Erase heading not required.)

C/73 R.F.A. 15 Div.

Instructions regarding War Diaries and Intelligence Summaries are contained in F. S. Regs., Part II. and the Staff Manual respectively. Title pages will be prepared in manuscript.

Place	Date	Hour	Summary of Events and Information	Remarks and references to Appendices
	JUNE			
	5.		Our fires on suspected M.G. emplacements in G.5.c. & retaliate fr. enemy firing minnows trenches in G.4.9. area.	Murder & Dawn [?] for day
	6.		Fairly quiet day - we registered M.G. emplacement & ret[urn] fire /or 4.2" heavy T.M.	45.
	7.		Quiet day -	37.
	8.		Unusually quiet -	12.
				8.

Ambrose Kay (?)
C/73 R.F.A.
(Crown)

73rd R.F.A.
Vol 11

Army Form C. 2118.

WAR DIARY
or
INTELLIGENCE SUMMARY.

73rd Bde R.F.A. (Erase heading not required.)

Month MAY 1916

Place	Date	Hour	Summary of Events and Information	Remarks and references to Appendices
BETHUNE	1st		15th Divisional R.A. Class begins under Lieut Col. C.S. Inglefield R.A.	Jn.S.
	2nd		Nothing to report	
	3rd		"	
	4th		"	
	5th		"	
	6th		"	
	7th		"	
	8th		"	
	9th		"	
	10th		"	
	11th		"	
	12th		"	
	13th		15th Divisional R.A. Class ends. Nothing to report	J.H.S.
	14th			
	15th		2'd 15th Divisional R.A. Class begins. Nothing to report.	J.H.S.
	16th			

Army Form C. 2118.

INTELLIGENCE SUMMARY.

73rd Bde R.F.A. *(Erase heading not required.)*

MAY 1916

Place	Date	Hour	Summary of Events and Information	Remarks and references to Appendices
BETHUNE	17th		nothing to report.	Ans
	18th		"	"
	19th		"	"
	20th		"	Ans.
	21st		73rd Bde. Am. Col. disbanded under new Art. reorganisation scheme	
	22nd		nothing to report	
	23rd		"	
	24th		"	
	25th		"	
	26th		"	Ans.
	27th		2nd 15th Divisional R.A. class "A" Sn. J's.	
	28th		nothing to report	
	29th		"	
	30th		"	
	31st		"	

[signature] Lt Col

3/5/16

WAR DIARY

D/73rd BRIGADE R. F. A.

May

1916.

Army Form C. 2118.

WAR DIARY
or
INTELLIGENCE SUMMARY. D/73

(Erase heading not required.)

Instructions regarding War Diaries and Intelligence Summaries are contained in F. S. Regs., Part II. and the Staff Manual respectively. Title pages will be prepared in manuscript.

Place	Date	Hour	Summary of Events and Information	Remarks and references to Appendices
Annequin	May 1st	-	Fairly Vigorous shelling. We retaliated on HOHENZOLLERN REDOUBT.	28 rounds
"	2"	-	Registered enemy Trenches. Quiet day.	27 "
"	3"	-	Retaliating for hostile shelling	37 "
"	4"	-	Bombarded enemy trenches	54 "
"	5"	-	Hostile artillery quite active. We retaliated.	122 "
"	6"	-	Still very active. We bombard trenches in retaliation.	207 "
"	7"	-	Called on to retaliate for heavy minenwerfers.	26 "
"	8"	-	Annequin heavily shelled	63 "
"	9"	-	Blew in several loopholes in craters	54 "
"	10"	-	Enemy's heavy minenwerfer firing from behind the DUMP.	62 "
"	11"	-	Huns attacked KINK and ANCHOR TRENCH after very fierce bombardment and occupied our front Support line on a front of 500 yds.	1041
"	12"	-	We bombarded enemy's new front line.	436.
"	13	-	A quiet day.	37.
"	14	-	A quiet day. We carried out a small bombardment.	609
"	15	-	A quiet day	nil.

T2134. Wt. W708-776. 500000. 4/15. Sir J. C. & S.

Army Form C. 2118.

WAR DIARY
or
INTELLIGENCE SUMMARY.   D/73

(Erase heading not required.)

2.

Instructions regarding War Diaries and Intelligence Summaries are contained in F. S. Regs., Part II. and the Staff Manual respectively. Title pages will be prepared in manuscript.

Place	Date	Hour	Summary of Events and Information	Remarks and references to Appendices
Annequin	May. 16.	.	A quiet day.	
.	17.	.	We bombarded HOHENZOLLERN REDOUBT, and answered heavy retaliation.	319
.	18.	.	A quiet day.	nil.
.	19.	.	Retaliated for a minenwerfer.	5.
.	20.	.	A quiet day.	16.
.	21.	.	We put up a barrage on enemy exploding a mine.	59.
.	22.	.	A quiet day	43.
.	23.	.	Enemy exploded a mine near the QUARRIES	73.
.	24.	.	A quiet day	56.
.	25.	.	Hostile minenwerfer very active. We barraged after blowing a mine.	49.
.	26.	.	Fired a loophole in conjunction with 18 hrs.	51.
.	27.	.	Fairly heavy shelling of our trenches	18.
.	28.	.	A quiet day.	26.
.	29.	.	A quiet day.	119.
.	30.	.	A quiet day.	16.
.	31.	.	A quiet day.	6.

A. A. Drew
for Major Comdg D/73

Army Form C. 2118.

WAR DIARY
or
INTELLIGENCE SUMMARY. (Erase heading not required.)

73rd Bde R.F.A.   JUNE 1916.

Place	Date	Hour	Summary of Events and Information	Remarks and references to Appendices
BETHUNE	1		} Nothing to report	} Ins.
	2			
	3			
	4			
	5			
	6		3rd 15th Divisional R.A Class begins	Ins.
	7	midnight	Reorganization scheme completed B/73, C/73, D/73 (How. Bty.) become respectively D/70, D/71	Ins.
	8		D/72 — D/70 D/71 D/72 (18 pdr Btys) become respectively B/73 C/73 D/73.	
	9			
	10			
	11		} Nothing to report	} Ins.
	12			
	13			
	14			
	15			
	16			

Army Form C. 2118.

73rd Bde R.F.A.

JUNE 1916. 73 RFA

Vol 12

WAR DIARY
or
INTELLIGENCE SUMMARY.

Place	Date	Hour	Summary of Events and Information	Remarks and references to Appendices
BETHUNE	17		3rd 15th Divisional R.A. class ends.	Ins.
	18			
	19			
	20			
	21			
	22			
"	23		Nothing to report	Ins.
	24			
	25			
	26			
	27			
	28			
	29			
	30			

W.H. Cooper
R.F.A.
Cmdg 73rd Bde R.F.A.

WAR DIARY

C/73rd BRIGADE R.F.A.

June

1916.

CONFIDENTIAL Army Form C. 2118

C/73 RFA for June 1916

e/73. 0 du RFA June

Vol 2

WAR DIARY
or
INTELLIGENCE SUMMARY
(Erase heading not required.)

Instructions regarding War Diaries and Intelligence Summaries are contained in F.S. Regs., Part II. and the Staff Manual respectively. Title Pages will be prepared in manuscript.

Place	Date	Hour	Summary of Events and Information	Remarks and references to Appendices
ANNEQUIN	7th to 17th June		Battery retaliated when required.	
do.	17th		Left section under Lieut. Lazarus went to be attached to B/70 R.F.A.; and C/85 came up to Annequin position & took over the fire zone.	
ANNEQUIN & VERMELLES	18th to 23rd		Battery retaliated when required. Wire cutting before Wire cut by left section near FC0 Quarries.	
do.	24th to 30th		Wire cutting and sundry strafes by both sections.	

R. F. Hand
Capt. R.F.A.
Comdg. C/73

C O N F I D E N T I A L.
========================

War Diary

73rd Bde RFA

From 1st to 31st July, 1916.

E Boyce
Major, R.A.
1st August, 1916.   Bde Major, 16th Divnl. Arty.

Army Form C. 2118.

WAR DIARY
or
INTELLIGENCE SUMMARY.
(Erase heading not required.)

73rd Bde R.F.A.   JULY 1916   73 RFA

Vol 13

Instructions regarding War Diaries and Intelligence Summaries are contained in F. S. Regs., Part II. and the Staff Manual respectively. Title pages will be prepared in manuscript.

Place	Date	Hour	Summary of Events and Information	Remarks and references to Appendices
BETHUNE	1		} Nothing to report.	
	2			
	3			
	4			
BETHUNE - PHILOSOPHE	5		Lt.Col. Ingham relieves Col Stirling (72nd Bde RFA) and takes over Command of RIGHT GROUP 15th D.A.	
PHILOSOPHE	6		RIGHT GROUP 15th D.A. (D/70(How) A/70 B/73 A/72 B/72 C/72 D/73) Enemy mildly active with "pipsqueaks" & "Minnies" & shells cross-roads at NOYELLES with 5.9". undertaken causing several casualties (military & civilian). B/73 reported several pits by aeroplane. at about 9 P.M. A/70 & B/73 opened fire in support of 16th Div. whose front was being heavily bombarded by the Huns. The Zone Hostile in the challenge was slightly damaged but the enemy was prevented from putting the trenches.	

WAR DIARY or INTELLIGENCE SUMMARY

Army Form C. 2118.

(3RD) RIGHT GROUP 15th A

JULY 1916

Place	Date	Hour	Summary of Events and Information	Remarks and references to Appendices
PHILOSOPHE	7		A few working parties tried on. 77mms apparently registering. T.M.s quiet.	
	8		A quiet day. No movement observed on work ditches. About 9 P.M. enemy made preparations for a raid, opening a heavy bombardment N & S of HULLUCH ROAD. Arty fire 1700 rds on right lines & STEELIE BARRAGE & curtailed his activity to the extent of a few rounds returning BRECON SAP.	
	9		D/170 (How) registered 6 pts, one by aeroplane. It was noticed that 77mm retaliation for 18 pdr Shelling was prompt and severe. A quiet day on the whole	
	10		Some enemy registration. Movement normal. 11.30 P.M. Rt group about 85-6 rounds in support of an successful raid carried out by b/14 I.B. above HOHENZOLLERN REDOUBT. We fired on 95 c	
	11.		2 P.M. - 6 P.M. Organised "Strafs" on G.12a & H.7.B.a respectively. These affected effective & enemy retaliation was very feeble. B & C/172 fired under aeroplane direction on a new system with a view to improving aeroplane co-operation with artillery when on the move. A few working parties "strafed" yesterday "strafs" repeated. Enemy very quiet; his retaliation was feeble.	
	12			

Army Form C. 2118.

WAR DIARY
or INTELLIGENCE SUMMARY.

RIGHT GROUP 15th (R.F.A.) JULY 1916

Place	Date	Hour	Summary of Events and Information	Remarks and references to Appendices
PHILOSOPHE	13		Some retaliation for enemy 77mm, & some working parties (shafts) A/70 claim to have killed 2 workers, 3 out of a party of 10. A quiet day.	
	14		A very quiet day. Only a few rounds fired in retaliation	
	15		Several working parties "strafed". Increased activity of MINNIES B/72 in retaliation to these Set PITS 13 on fire, it was burning in smoke for some time. Night) 14/15 C/72 came out of action & joined CONCHY in smoke for some time. Night) 14/15 C/72 came out of action & joined CONCHY GROUP	
	16		From noon an exchange of strafes was carried out which lasted until the morning of 17th. Trenches in GSc were heard shelled during afternoon, & during the night an intermittent 'strafe' was kept up on the enemies' Communication trenches all his trench tramway Junctions. 265 rds of how ammunition were fired + 225 4.5", 18 pdr ammunition.	
	17		Enemy fairly active with 77's on left front. Some 77's Shrenny retaliates work (no effect. Between 8.30 PM + 9 PM Lutz opened a heavy fire with 77's as well. We fired some 650 rds on BORDER REDOUBT Barrage. No infantry action, we caused a fire in their Redoubt.	

Army Form C. 2118.

WAR DIARY
or
INTELLIGENCE SUMMARY.

73 R.G.A.
RIGHT GROUP 15th S.B.

JULY 1916

Place	Date	Hour	Summary of Events and Information	Remarks and references to Appendices
PROSOPHE	18	2 P.M.	until morning of 19th — Strafe of 16th repeats, 200 rds Hun ammunition & 2159 rds of 18 pdr ammunition used.	
	19.		A/70 fired 328 rds in co-operation with 16th Divisional Raid. Noon to 3.50 P.M. Registration & Bombardment. 9 Hun trenches in G.5.C. Two Walinta Straffs with 77mm & some 4.2's opposite front bombers(?). We fired 130 Hun rounds & about 1000 rds 18 pdr ammunition.	
	20	8.25 P.M.	A/73 successfully drove off 2 hostile aeroplanes which were flying very low over the QUARRIES. Enemy very quiet except for a few 77's & MINNIES which were promptly retaliated on. One working party fired on.	
	21.		A very quiet day. Less movement than usual. We retaliated to a few 77's & an occasional MINNIE. 3 working parties dispersed.	
	22.		Very quiet — A (our) day for observation owing to haze. A/as 77's and a MINNIE was retaliated for ----- 11.30 P.M.	

Army Form C. 2118.

WAR DIARY
or
INTELLIGENCE SUMMARY.
(Erase heading not required.)

Army Troops, 1st Army JULY 1916

R.F.A. Group

Place	Date	Hour	Summary of Events and Information	Remarks and references to Appendices
HALLOY	22	11.30 P.M.	A section of 4 inch Hy. in the group was relieved. A section of 16 S.A. Section of 73rd Bde moved to EPS night of 22/23.	
	23		Remainder of R.T. Group Btys relieved. Remaining Sections of 73rd Bde moved to EPS night of 23/24. 73rd Bde H.Q. Staff moves to EPS. 73rd Bde, R.F.A.	
	24		73rd Bde. rested at EPS.	
	25			
	26		73rd Bde. moved from EPS to CONCHY-SUR-CANCHE.	
	27		73rd Bde. moved from CONCHY-SUR-CANCHE to MÉZEROLLES.	
	28		73rd Bde. moved from MÉZEROLLES to HARDINVAL.	
	29		73rd Bde. rested at HARDINVAL. Drills carried out under battery arrangements.	
	30		73rd Bde rested at HARDINVAL. Drills carried out under battery arrangements.	
	31		73rd Bde ordered to BETHINCOURT-ST-OUEN.	

[signature]
31/7/16
73rd R.F.A.

15th Divisional Artillery

73rd BRIGADE

ROYAL FIELD ARTILLERY

AUGUST 1 9 1 6

CONFIDENTIAL.

WAR DIARY.

of

73rd Brigade, R.F.A.

From 1st August, 1916   to   31st August, 1916.

VOLUME Number 14

E. Boyce

Major, R.A.
Brigade Major R.A., 15th Divisional Artillery.

Army Form C. 2118.

73 RFA
Vol 14

WAR DIARY
or
INTELLIGENCE SUMMARY.
(Erase heading not required.)

73rd Bde R.F.A.   AUGUST 1916

Place	Date	Hour	Summary of Events and Information	Remarks and references to Appendices
BETHINCOURT	1.		73rd Bde rests at BETHINCOURT-ST-OUEN	
ST OUEN → BEAUCOURT	2.		73rd Bde moves from BETHINCOURT-ST-OUEN to BEAUCOURT. M. Ingham & Bty Commanders sent on a reconnaissance of the positions to be taken over by the 73rd Bde.	
	3.		Night of 3/4th 1 Section per battery of 73rd Bde relieves corresponding Sections of 86th Bde R.F.A. 19th D.A. in positions behind BAZENTIN-LE-GRAND. 1 gunner A/73 wounded 4/8/16.	
	4		Night of 4/5th remaining Sections of 73rd Bde & Bde H.Q. complete relief of 86th Bde. Bde H.Q being a few yds from A battery. A battery took over only one gun, the others being in the shops. B & C took over complete but throughout the Bde many inner springs and parting plates were broken and in nearly every case the remaining springs were much compressed.	
BAZENTIN	4/5			
	5		73rd Bde barrages with a view to installing INTERMEDIATE line W of HIGH WOOD (in S.3.c & d), when not firing all batteries	

Army Form C. 2118.

WAR DIARY
or
INTELLIGENCE SUMMARY

73rd Bde R.F.A. AUGUST 1916.

Place	Date	Hour	Summary of Events and Information	Remarks and references to Appendices
BAZENTIN	5		were employed in digging, in order to render their positions more secure in the event of being heavily "straped".	
"	6		INTERMEDIATE line & digging operations continued. 1 Gunner killed A/73.	
"	7		1 Corporal & 7 men wounded by a shell at B battery's wagon line at Becourt. One shell which also set fire to an ammunition wagon. The ammunition was saved with the exception of two rounds owing to the presence of mind of Cpl Burnley, Gnr Harding Btbr Bromley & Gnr Smallwood. Same firing programme continued. Bde H.Q. moved back to just in front of MAMETZ.	
MAMETZ	8		1 Gunner wounded in A Bty. Same programme continued. Special "strap" for the same purpose at night.	

Army Form C. 2118.

WAR DIARY
or
INTELLIGENCE SUMMARY. August 1916.
73rd Bde R.F.A.
(Erase heading not required.)

Place	Date	Hour	Summary of Events and Information	Remarks and references to Appendices
MAMETZ	9		Barrage D. A quiet day.	
	10		A quiet day. Area round A Bty shelled with 4.2s about 10 P.M.	
	11		1 Gunner of B wounded. B + C intermittently shelled with 77 mm	
	12		1 Gunner of A wounded	
	13		Nothing to report	
	14		Barrage H substituted for Barrage D. A/73 heavily bombarded in the morning with 5.9", 4.2". 1 Sgt of A + 1 Bdr 7/3 wounded.	
	15		Barrage H. A quiet day. Boche planes abnormally active during the evening	
	16		Barrage H. MARTINPUICH CHURCH registered by balloon. A very quiet day on our front. At 10 P.M. in conjunction with 71st + 72nd Bdes the Brigade supported the 2nd I.B. in a successful surprise attack on part of the INTERMEDIATE TRENCH. 1 Sgt + 2 Gunners of B bty wounded & 1 Gr in C	
	17		A quiet day. At 6.15 P.M. the Enemy opened a heavy fire on back side of Bn front. All Btys turned on to Barrage H until 6.45 P.M.	

WAR DIARY
INTELLIGENCE SUMMARY

73rd Bde R.F.A.   AUGUST 1916

Place: MAMETZ

Date	Hour	Summary of Events and Information
17		
18	4pm	[Guns in action A.3. B+C & Back] Lt Chamberlayne killed at B Bty by Shell which burst 200 yds away. A Bdr was also wounded at the same time. In the afternoon at 2.45 a successful attack was made on N.W. corner of HIGH WOOD.
19		Barrage on SWITCH LINE. Later information says that some of our men are in a near SWITCH LINE. Barrage lifted beyond SWITCH LINE. Situation by no means clear.
20		Enemy attack on N.W. corner of HIGH WOOD. Our men now said not to be N.W. corner of HIGH WOOD. Information very different. Hostile situation not yet clear. 1 gun NR9 I driver of A wounded. Several enemy counter attacks. Now definitely stated that our men are not in the SWITCH LINE but have a post at S.36.c.3. SWITCH LINE bombed.
21		B Bty Wagon line bombarded 2 drivers & killing 2 horses. I horse also wounded. Luckily the main part of the men & horses were

Army Form C. 2118.

WAR DIARY or INTELLIGENCE SUMMARY.
(Erase heading not required.)

73rd T.M. Bde (R.F.A)   AUGUST 1916

Place	Date	Hour	Summary of Events and Information	Remarks and references to Appendices
MAMETZ	21		On practice some 300 yds away or more casualties would undoubtedly have resulted. Barrage of Shrabnels too inaccurate.	
	22		A quiet day.	
	23		A few heavy shells during the evening	
	24		3.45 AM to about 7.30 a heavy shoot was in progress but not on our front. On our left an unsuccessful attack was made on the rest of the INTERMEDIATE TRENCH which on our right was attacked in direction of DELVILLE WOOD & GUILLEMONT. Heavy shelling of B+C with 5.9 & 8" A.P. during afternoon. Capt Nelson's dugout blown in on him. (A Macey evacuated with Shellshock) 2 Gunners Smiths wounded. 2 more dugouts of B Bty & signal dugouts of C blown in - all 2nd Lt. McDonough in the 5th dugout - and flying communication were interrupted, wires & killed.	
	25		4 Sept, the A.O.D. sept to a fm were interrupted, wires & killed. During the night of 25/26 B+C moved their positions to the rear of A Bty. Owing to shelling very from work was done by the Bde Signallers & R.E. by their pluck & Energy kept communication with these batteries & at all short periods	

Army Form C. 2118.

WAR DIARY
or
INTELLIGENCE SUMMARY. AUGUST 1916

(Erase heading not required.)

73rd Bde RFA

Place	Date	Hour	Summary of Events and Information	Remarks and references to Appendices
MAMETZ	26		A quiet day until evening, when from 7 – 9.30 P.M. the Bty area was heavily shelled with 8" A.P. 1 gun of B Bty was destroyed by a direct hit. 2 of the detachment being killed and 2 wounded. During the night of 26/27 B Bty moved to the other side of C Bty. 1 Cpl B wounded by a shrapnel.	
	27		A quiet day. 1 Bdr of C wounded	
	28		A quiet day. 1 Gnr of C wounded	
	29		A quiet day. 1 Gnr of B injured.	
	30		Heavy rain. Observation almost impossible owing to bad weather conditions. Always subjected to harassing fire systematically destroying batteries with aid of	
	31		536 9½.5 – S3 f 4.8. to be supplemented by A/73, B/73 + B/71. C/73's Communications continually broken + change of O.P. necessitated.	

Ammunition Expended during Month :-
30,437 A + 14,689 AX.

[signature] Lt Col

Comd. 73 RFA
31/8/16

Lulu 20-16

V(9/15

Army Form C. 2118.

WAR DIARY
or
INTELLIGENCE SUMMARY.
(Erase heading not required.)

73rd Bde R.F.A   SEPTEMBER 1916

Place	Date	Hour	Summary of Events and Information	Remarks and references to Appendices
MAMETZ	1.		Battery area shelled with 'lethal shells' during night of 31/1. 1 gun of A evacuated gassed. 10-12 A Bty heavily shelled with 5.9's. 1 gun damaged. The removal of the bty necessitated the position without casualties, but the position was destroyed and A bty moved its position into MARLBOROUGH COPSE. Destruction of trench S 36 5 9½ – S 36 4 8 continued satisfactorily by B+C/73 + B/71. 1 Sect B/73 relieved by 1 Sect. C170 on night of 1/2.	Ap?
	2.		Battery area again shelled with 'lethal shells' during night of 9 1/2. These were also interspersed with 5.9's. Our exceptionally quiet day Area N 9 HIGH WOOD to be searched intermittently + methodically by 73rd Bde up to ZERO HOUR of the attack to be made by 1st Division on 3/9/1916. This was started at 1 P.M. 1Sgt + 1 gnr of C wounded. 1 Sect B/73 relieved by 1 sect C/70 on night of 9 2½/3	Ap?
	3.		A quiet morning. At 12 NOON (ZERO HOUR) the Bde. Supported 1st Dril attack on WOOD LANE after 3 P.M. a barrage was kept up on N½ of HIGH WOOD. Besides this F.O.O's turned then fires on the Boche as they counter attacked + did good execution when opportunity offered. The 1st attack was at first successful, but our troops were later driven back.	Ap?

WAR DIARY
INTELLIGENCE SUMMARY.

73rd Bde RFA September 1916

Place	Date	Hour	Summary of Events and Information	Remarks and references to Appendices
MAMETZ	4		Enemy very quiet. About 5.30 P.M. Several hostile aeroplanes taking advantage of the absence of any of our Planes all over the back area for some 20 minutes, by which time our Airmen appeared & the enemy machines withdrew. At 3 P.M. a "Chinese attack" was carried out, the Bde firing "intense fire" for 4½ minutes.	AJJ
	5		An abnormally quiet day.	
	6.		Very quiet on our front. Shrap in direction of DELVILLE WOOD was heard in the evening.	AJJ
	7.		A quiet day.	
	8.		6 P.M. Fired in support of attack on trench running out of N.W. Corner of HIGH WOOD, in conjunction with an attack by the division on our right. The attack was successful. A counter attack was caught by our barrage, but our men eventually had to retire owing to the division on our right falling back.	

Army Form C. 2118.

WAR DIARY
or
INTELLIGENCE SUMMARY.
(Erase heading not required.)

73rd Bde R.F.A.   SEPTEMBER 1916

Place	Date	Hour	Summary of Events and Information	Remarks and references to Appendices
MAMETZ	9	4.45 P.M.	Barrage to cover attack on HIGH WOOD in conjunction with operations of the division on our right. Situation obscure.	
	10		In afternoon (3 P.M.) A Section of A/73 C/73 reps moved into positions near PEAKE WOOD corresponding Sections of 252 Bde R.F.A. coming into our positions. At 12 noon the Bde came temporarily under orders of 50th D.A. A quiet day.	
PEAKE WOODS	11.	9.30 A.M.	Renewing sections of batteries. Exchanged positions with 252nd Bde R.F.A. Bde H.Q. moved to X 22 a ½ 6.	
		12 Noon	Bde became responsible for new part of line and guns came under orders of 15 D.A. B/70 now under Command. A/73. X16c52. C/73. X22a61. D/78 X 22 a 6 5. D/70 X 22 a 2 2	
	12.		A quiet day. Positions A/73.	
	13.		ditto.	
	14.		B/71 (X 10 to 6.0.) Came under orders of 73 R.F.A.	
	15	6.20 A.M.	ZERO HOUR. Began firing as ordered. The barrage appeared effective, the lifts being well together and keeping just ahead of the infantry, who suffered no casualties from the barrage.	

WAR DIARY
INTELLIGENCE SUMMARY.
(Erase heading not required.)

73rd Bde R.F.A.

SEPTEMBER 1916.

Army Form C. 2118.

Place	Date	Hour	Summary of Events and Information	Remarks and references to Appendices
PEAKE WOODS	15th			
		6.30am	Enemy's reply was very feeble, consisting of only a few 5·9's. The "tanks" were very successful + caused great consternation amongst the Bosches. Prisoners began arriving.	
		7.20am	Prisoners reported Coming in from MARTINPUICH.	
		7.30am	Tanks reported to have reached and strafed at FACTORY LINE.	
		7.20am	Argylls reported digging in 50x N of Div. boundary.	
		7.50am	Everything reported to have gone according to schedule, and our infantry to be holding their objectives.	
		8 Am	Tanks began return journey.	
		8.57 am	Enemy reported to be evacuating GUNPITTR, and some back to ridge in M 26.	
		9 Am	Enemy Sausage brought down in flames (2nd was brought down later in the day)	
		9.15am	MARTINPUICH appears to be evacuated also ridge N from M 25 d 5.4. to M 27 c 1.7 (in action 11.30 A.M.)	
		9.45 am	A/73 ordered to move up to X 12 a 1.2.	

Army Form C. 2118.

WAR DIARY
or
INTELLIGENCE SUMMARY.
(Erase heading not required.)

73rd Bde. R.F.A. September 1916

Place	Date	Hour	Summary of Events and Information	Remarks and references to Appendices
PEAKE WOODS	15	10.10 am	By fire started in MARTIN PUICH.	
		10.45 am	Hostile bty at M 21 c.6.5. Engaged by C/73 (reported by wireless)	
		11. A.M	" " " M 21 c 3.5. " B/71	
			" " " " A/73	
		12.30 P.M	" " M 21 d 6.7 " "	
		11.30 A.M.	C/70 moved forward to X.11.b.6.9.3. and D/70 to X 17 c 15.5 (in action 12.30 PM)	
		5.30 P.M	Hostile btys at M 21 b 3.5. + M 21 d 6.7. Engaged by B/71 + A/73 respectively.	
		6.10 P.M	Hostile bty at M 21 d 7.6. Engaged by C/73	
		6.20 P.M	Canadians appeared to be attacking on our left. The enemy put up a wild barrage on POZIERES and trenches around it, using shell of all calibres.	
		6.25 P.M	A/73 Engaged hostile btys at M 21 d 6.7. and M 21 b 5.5.	
		7 P.M	C/70 engaged a hostile bty nw corner of q action at M 21 c 8.3. At no time during the day did the enemy put on a really effective barrage. Although at times thrown over an enormous quantity of heavy shell all his fire was mild, The night was quiet.	
	16.		Hostile btys in M 21 d 6.7 + M 21. b 3.8 engaged during the day. It is believed	

WAR DIARY
or
INTELLIGENCE SUMMARY

73rd Bde. R.F.A.   September 1916

Place	Date	Hour	Summary of Events and Information	Remarks and references to Appendices
PRIZE WOODS	16		Fire was effective as these Btys. were not again reporting active Enemy shells. MARTINPUICH & COURCELETTE almost continually with heavy howrs from direction of WARLENCOURT-FAVREUIL + PYS with 8" + 5.9's with a few 4.2's between 6.30 p.m. & 7 p.m. his fire became intense but he did not show himself. The enemy's infantry was quiet, our men digging their new front line in broad daylight unmolested.	
	17.		A quiet day.	
	18.		Mist and rain all day. Observation poor. Enemy barraged CONTALMAISON with 8" H.A.P. and 5.9" from 4.30 p.m. to 5 p.m. 1 Section of A/73 and C/73 were relieved by 1 section of A/72 and B/73 respectively during the evening.	
	19.		A very quiet day. Reliefs complete, & H.Q. letters by 71st Bde H.Q. Bde went to rest at ST GRATIEN.	
ST GRATIEN	20			
	21, 22, 23, 24, 25, 26, 27, 28, 29, 30.		Bde (H.Q. A/73, A/73 & C/73 (Return with A/71 & C/71 attached) arrived 30th Sept. Bde turn out" inspection. Won by C/73. 30.9.16	[signature] Lt.Col. 73. 30.9.16

CONFIDENTIAL.

War Diary

of

73rd Bde RFA

1st October, 1916.   to   31st October, 1916.

VOLUME. 16.

Major R.A.

Brigade Major 15th Divisional Arty.

Army Form C. 2118.

WAR DIARY
or
INTELLIGENCE SUMMARY.

Vol 16

73rd Bde R.F.A.

OCTOBER 1916.

Place	Date	Hour	Summary of Events and Information	Remarks and references to Appendices
ST GRATIEN	1st		During the month of September the following distinctions were won in the Bde. 1 D.C.M. 21 Military Medals	
	2nd		Bde (A/73, C/73, A/71, C/71) at rest at ST GRATIEN. Sections of A/73 + C/73 relieved sections of A/70 + C/70 at BAZENTIN-LE-PETIT.	
ST GRATIEN – BAZENTIN – LE-PETIT	3rd		Remaining sections of A/73 + C/73 which remaining sections of A/70 + C/70. B/73 moved over to position of B/70. Bde H.Q. took over from H.Q. 70th Bde, the Bde being again mild. Rain + mist, a very quiet day.	
BAZENTIN -LE-PETIT	4	5.30 P.M.	Still misty. O.G. 2 (S.W. of LE SARS) barraged in support of an attack by the infantry. Barrage lifted + infantry went over at 6.8 P.M.	

Army Form C. 2118.

WAR DIARY
or
INTELLIGENCE SUMMARY.
(Erase heading not required.)

Instructions regarding War Diaries and Intelligence Summaries are contained in F. S. Regs., Part II. and the Staff Manual respectively. Title pages will be prepared in manuscript.

Place	Date	Hour	Summary of Events and Information	Remarks and references to Appendices
BAZENTIN LE PETIT.	5		A quiet day. Misty & damp. Nothing to report. Registration carried out for an attack on LE SARS.	RW
	6		MARTINPUICH, LE SARS and EAUCOURT L'ABBAYE were shelled all day by 77mm guns.	
	7		About noon the enemy barraged LE SARS (on King) very heavily with 77mm fire shells	RW
		1.45.	At 1.45pm an attack was made on LE SARS. Our fire concentrates on the left flank barrage & barrage for 69th Bde as scheduled.	
		3.0pm	Barraged Quarry & road running SE from M57.c.0.9.	
		3.50	Barrage shifts lower down the road.	
		4.40.	Section turned on to M15 Central where enemy reported massing.	
		5.30.	Another battery turned on to M15 Central.	
		6.45.	Rose shaped barrage in M5.a. This was continued all night.	
		—	It was noticeable during the day that whenever our heavy batteries shelled enemy batteries a considerable number of them were seen straggling back across the open to trenches & dug outs in M5C&D.	

1577 Wt. W10791/1773 500,000 1/15 D.D.& L. A.D.S.S./Forms/C. 2118.

Army Form C. 2118.

WAR DIARY
or
INTELLIGENCE SUMMARY.
(Erase heading not required.)

Place	Date	Hour	Summary of Events and Information	Remarks and references to Appendices
BAZENTIN LE PETIT	8.		Flank barrage as ordered from MgC70 to MgC5.5. in support of an attack on the Quarry & Chalk Pit in M.15.6.	RW
	9.		Barrage continued all day as ordered. A quiet day barrage carried on as ordered. About 100 Boche reported still hiding as to dugout in M.18.C. Gurkhas propose starving him out.	RW
	10		During the afternoon the enemy began a lively bombardment on the valley the left of HOOK TR with S.g. Bombardment carried out as ordered. H.E. reported bursting badly owing to soft ground. Sections of B & C batteries moved to forward positions at dusk.	RW
	11.		Heavy Bombardment of MARTINPUICH at about 4p.m. Bombardment & Chinese attack carried out as ordered. B/73 & C/73 completed their moves & A/73 moved as section forward to S3.	RW

Army Form C. 2118.

WAR DIARY
or
INTELLIGENCE SUMMARY.
(Erase heading not required.)

Instructions regarding War Diaries and Intelligence Summaries are contained in F. S. Regs., Part II. and the Staff Manual respectively. Title pages will be prepared in manuscript.

Place	Date	Hour	Summary of Events and Information	Remarks and references to Appendices
BAZENTIN LE PETIT.	12		Intermittent shelling of MARTINPUICH and EAUCOURT L'ABBAYE also the trenches in M9b, M22a, M33c, both 15 cwt shell between 11.10 am	[initials]
		4.15 pm	Occasional bursts of fire on road in M27c. We engaged suspected OP in M14A. During an attack this afternoon by 9th Div. the Brigade carried out barrages as ordered. A/73 (more) remaining section to PRUE COPSE at dusk. Hostile Arty more active than usual. MARTINPUICH, DESTREMONT FARM, EAUCOURT L'ABBAYE & FLERS receiving considerable attention	
	13.		from 4.2 & 5.9s. One section of A/73 cut wire in front of SNOWITZ TR the other section consolidated its new position in PRUE COPSE which received slight attention from a (five) pipsqueak battery.	[initials]
	14		A dull & quiet day. Observation poor. Hostile Artillery activity below normal. The Brigade fired barrages as ordered. Three Hun observation balloons up during the day.	[initials]
	15.		Observation poor. Barrages carried out as ordered. Considerable hostile aeroplane & observation balloon activity	[initials]

Army Form C. 2118.

WAR DIARY
or
INTELLIGENCE SUMMARY.

(Erase heading not required.)

Place	Date	Hour	Summary of Events and Information	Remarks and references to Appendices
BAZENTIN LE PETIT.	16.		A quiet day. Very little hostile Arty activity. Visibility excellent but no hostile movement detected. Great aerial activity on both sides. Barrage carried out as ordered.	N/S.
	17.		A quiet day. Intermittent hostile shelling of EAUCOURT l'ABBAYE + LE SARS. Slight movement was noticed on LE SARS – BAPAUME Road. Barrage carried out as ordered. Registration of SW outskirts of PYS by Hy/3 Light toc bas for further registrations. II/70 rejoins the 70th Bde. 113th Siege Bty joins 73rd Bde at midnight.	N/S.
	18.	3.30pm	A successful attack on a trench in front BUTTE was supported by this Bde. Fairly heavy bombardment of EAUCOURT l'ABBAYE. 60 pdrs bombarded WARLENCOURT, LOUPART Wood & LITTLE Wood. Good work being done. Barrages to carried out as ordered.	N/S.
	19.		Bad weather and a quiet day.	
	20.		A quiet day, barrages carried out as ordered.	
	21.		The Bde. Supported a successful attack by the Canadians on REGINA TRENCH. Enemy massing for a counter	

WAR DIARY or INTELLIGENCE SUMMARY

Army Form C. 2118.

Place	Date	Hour	Summary of Events and Information	Remarks and references to Appendices
BAZENTIN-LE-PETIT.	22		attack near PYS were also successfully engaged. A/73 moved their backward section up in front of their	
	23		PRUE COPSE section, which B+C/73 pushed a gun back forward. These moves were completed on the night 22/23rd.	
	24 25		WARLENCOURT, LITTLE WOOD + LOUPART WOOD Bombarded. Barrages as ordered + movements (containing enemy) Bde supports unsuccessful attack by Corps on our Left.	
	26		A quiet day.	
	27 28		The Bde. relieved by 71st Bde RFA on the 27th/28th. Bde moved back to rest at ST GRATIEN.	
	29 30 31		Bde at Rest at ST GRATIEN. Rds fired during month 46,000.	

During October the Bde won the following distinctions 4 Military Crosses (Capt. Hanna, Capt. Graham, A. Hatton, H. Mason) 1 Military Medal, 2 Meritorious Service medals.
3 men were wounded during the month.

31/10/16.

[signature]

S.D.A

Herewith War Diary
for 73rd Bde R.F.A for November
1916

Chrystie

30-11-16   Cmdg 73rd Bde R.F.A

C O N F I D E N T I A L.

War Diary.

of

73 Bde R.F.A.

From 1st November, 1916 — 30th November, 1916.

VOLUME 17

1.11.16.

Gallagher
Captain,
for Bde Major 15th Divisional Arty.

Army Form C. 2118.

WAR DIARY
or
INTELLIGENCE SUMMARY.
(Erase heading not required.)

Vol 17

73rd Bde R.F.A

NOVEMBER 1916

Place	Date	Hour	Summary of Events and Information	Remarks and references to Appendices
ST GRATIEN	1st – 8th		Bde at Rest at ST GRATIEN.	
	8th/9th		Bde returned to line taking over from 72nd Bde R.F.A.	
MIDDLE WOOD	9th		Bde H.Q at MIDDLE WOOD. Reps in S.3. with 1 Section of B/73 formed at M 33 c 99. Bde un'r Command of 50th D.A. D/72 taken over tactically by O.C. 73rd Bde R.F.A.	
	10th	3.15 P.M.	Special Bombardment of GALLWITZ LINE	
	11th	9.10 A.M	Special Bombardment of GALLWITZ LINE	
	12th	12.5 PM	" " " & COUPE TRENCH.	
	13th	8.15 AM	" " "	
		9.45 AM	" " "	
		5.45 AM	CHINESE ATTACK (GALLWITZ TRENCH, WARLENCOURT ETC) in aid of Attack by 5th ARMY – [5th ARMY took BEAUMONT-HAMEL & later BEAUCOURT-SUR-ANCRE while CANADIANS took ST PIERRE DIVION & & linked up with them.]	
	14th		Concentrated Bombardment of WARLENCOURT by 4.5" Hows on night of 14th/15th – 23rd D.A. take over LINE.	

Army Form C. 2118.

WAR DIARY or INTELLIGENCE SUMMARY.

(Erase heading not required.)

73rd Bde R.F.A.   NOVEMBER 1916.

Place	Date	Hour	Summary of Events and Information	Remarks and references to Appendices
HIDDLEWOOD	15		NIGHT 15th/16th LOUPART WOOD "shape's"	
	16		A quiet day.	
	17	5 P.M. to MIDNIGHT	An increased rate of fire on NIGHT BARRAGE	
			owing to believed GERMAN relief.	
	18	6.10 A.M.	CHINESE ATTACK on normal fronts (GREWITZ LINE etc.)	
	19	10.30 A.M.	Bde takes over new zone. New zone stretches from the	
			LE SARS — BAPAUME RD at t.L. to just about 50x R. of the	
			BUTTE - DE - WARLENCOURT.	
	20		A quiet day. Night firing as ordered. Under new	
			system of night firing. Certain rounds on front. net fired on	
			for some night but trusting enemy to try use them, then shifted heavy	
			one night.	
			LOUPART WOOD shapes with gas shell during night.	
	21		A quiet day. Short bursts of fire kept up during night.	
	22		Nothing to report.	
	23			
	24			

Army Form C. 2118.

WAR DIARY
or
INTELLIGENCE SUMMARY.
(Erase heading not required.)

73rd Bde R.F.A.   NOVEMBER 1916

Place	Date	Hour	Summary of Events and Information	Remarks and references to Appendices
MIDDLE WOOD	25		Rain all day & light v. from. Practically no firing all day. At 4.25 f the Enemy sent up numerous red lights each mouth into town along the whole front from PYS to GUEDECOURT but nothing followed. Misty till day – no firing	
"	26		— " — Increase of Enemy Shelling	
	27th		— " — Practically no Shelling again.	
	28th		— " — " Shelling by Enemy	
	29th		— " — Very little Shelling by Ener. the Sheffer	
	31st		A little Enemy Shelling Etc. all day. No Raids Snipers Etc. all day	Attach

30-11-16

Whytehouse
Major
Comdg 73rd Bde R.F.A.

Confidential

Herewith War Diary of
73rd Bde R.F.A.

Ashyman

3/12/16   Cmdg 73 rd Bde R.F.A.

Vol 18

WAR DIARY
or
INTELLIGENCE SUMMARY.

Army Form C. 2118.

War Diary 73rd Bde R.F.A. DECEMBER September 1916

Place	Date	Hour	Summary of Events and Information	Remarks and references to Appendices
MIDDLE Wood	1/12/16		At midnight 30-11-16 – 1.12-16 The 73rd Bde was made into 2 Six gun Batteries, 1E A/73 Sent 1 Section to each, B/73 and C/73.	Attn
	2/12/16		Very quiet day. Enemy seemed to be a little more active with his H.28's, they made most use of two Heavy Guns. He shelled the Rover & Trones all day. And fired at a working Party out/around near the BUTTE	
	3/12/16		Night, unable to sleep. At 1 a.m. the 73rd Bde ceased to Exist. B/73 being posted as G/71 to 71st Bde R.F.A. C/73 to 76th Bde do & D/70. I, Lt. Col. C. ST. M. INGHAM on vacating command of 73rd Bde assume command of 91 S. Bde. R.F.A	

Wykeham
Comdg 73 73rd Bde R.F.A.

www.ingramcontent.com/pod-product-compliance
Lightning Source LLC
Chambersburg PA
CBHW081551160426
43191CB00011B/1900